SIMPLICITY
IN
PREACHING

A Guide to Powerfully Communicating
God's Word

by
J. C. Ryle

Printed on acid free ANSI archival quality paper.
ISBN: 978-1-78139-888-3.
© 2017 Benediction Classics, Oxford.

If you want to attain simplicity in preaching:

1. Have a clear knowledge of what you are going to preach.

2. Use simple words.

3. Use a simple style of composition, with short sentences and as few colons and semicolons as possible.

4. Be direct.

5. Make abundant use of illustration and anecdote.

Finally, all the simplicity in the world is useless without the outpouring of the Holy Spirit. Remember to accompany your sermon with holy living and fervent prayer.

Simplicity in Preaching

King Solomon says, in the book of Ecclesiastes, "Of making many books there is no end" (12:12). There are few subjects about which that saying is more true than that of preaching. The volumes which have been written in order to show ministers how to preach are enough to make a small library. In sending forth one more little treatise, I only propose to touch one branch of the subject. I do not pretend to consider what should be the substance and matter of a sermon. I purposely leave alone such points as "gravity, unc- tion, liveliness, warmth," and the like, or the comparative merits of written or extemporaneous sermons. I wish to confine myself to one point, which receives far less attention than it deserves. That point is **simplicity in language and style**.

I ought to be able to tell my readers something about "simplici- ty," if experience will give any help. I began preaching forty-five years ago, when I first took orders in a poor rural parish, and a great portion of my ministerial life has been spent in preaching to laborers and farmers. I know the enormous difficulty of preaching to such hearers, of making them understand one's meaning, and securing their attention. So far as concerns language and composi- tion, I deliberately say that I would rather preach before the University at Oxford or Cambridge, or the Temple, or Lincoln's Inn, or the Houses of Parliament, than I would address an agricul- tural congregation on a fine hot afternoon in the month of August. I have heard of a laborer who enjoyed Sunday more than any other day in the week, "Because," he said, "I sit comfortably in church, put up my legs, have nothing to think about, and just go to sleep." Some of my younger friends in the ministry may some day be called to preach to such congregations as I have had, and I shall be glad if they can profit by my experience.

PREFATORY REMARKS

Before entering on the subject, I wish to clear the way by making four prefatory remarks.

1. For one thing, I ask all my readers to remember that **to attain simplicity in preaching is of the utmost importance to every minister who wishes to be useful to souls**. Unless you are simple in your sermons you will never be understood, and unless you are understood you cannot do good to those who hear you. It was a true saying of Quintilian, "If you do not wish to be understood, you deserve to be neglected." Of course the first object of a minister should be to preach the truth, the whole truth, and nothing but "the truth as it is in Jesus." But the next thing he ought to aim at is, that his sermon may be understood; and it will not be understood by most of his hearers if it is not simple.

2. The next thing I will say, by way of prefatory remark, is, that **to attain simplicity in preaching is by no means an easy matter**. No greater mistake can be made than to suppose this. "To make hard things seem hard," to use the substance of a saying of Archbishop Usher's, "is within the reach of all, but to make hard things seem easy and intelligible is a height attained by very few speakers." One of the wisest and best of the Puritans said two hundred years ago, "that the greater part of preachers shoot over the heads of the people." This is true also in 1837! I fear a vast proportion of what we preach is not understood by our hearers any more than if it were Greek. When people hear a simple sermon, or read a simple tract, they are apt to say, "How true! how plain! how easy to understand!" and to suppose that any one can write in that

style. Allow me to tell my readers that **it is an extremely difficult thing to write simple, clear, perspicuous, and forcible English**. Look at the sermons of Charles Bradley, of Clapham. A sermon of his reads most beautifully. It is so simple and natural, that anyone feels at once that the meaning is as clear as the sun at noonday. **Every word is the right word, and every word is in its right place.** Yet the labor those sermons cost Mr. Bradley was very great indeed. Those who have read Goldsmith's Vicar of Wakefield attentively, can hardly fail to have noticed the exquisite naturalness, ease, and simplicity of its language. And yet it is known that the pains and trouble and time bestowed upon that work were immense. Let the Vicar of Wakefield be compared with Johnson's Rasselas, which was written off in a few days, it is said, under higher pressure—and the difference is at once apparent. In fact, to use very long words, to seem very learned, to make people go away after a sermon saying, "How fine! how clever! how grand!" all this is very easy work. But to write what will strike and stick, to speak or to write that which at once pleases and is understood, and becomes assimilated with a hearer's mind and a thing never forgotten—that, we may depend upon it, is a very difficult thing and a very rare attainment.

3. Let me observe, in the next place, that when I talk of simplicity in preaching, **I would not have my readers suppose I mean childish preaching**. If we suppose the poor like that sort of sermon, we are greatly mistaken. If our hearers once imagine we consider them a parcel of ignorant folks for whom any kind of "infant's food" is good enough, our chance of doing good is lost altogether. People do not like even the appearance of 'condescending preaching'. They feel we are not treating them as equals, but inferiors. Human nature always dislikes that. They will at once put up their backs, stop their ears, and take offence—and then we might as well preach to the winds.

4. Finally, let me observe, that **it is not coarse or vulgar preaching that is needed**. It is quite possible to be simple, and

yet to speak like a gentleman, and with the demeanor of a courteous and refined person. It is an utter mistake to imagine that uneducated and illiterate men and women prefer to be spoken to in an illiterate way, and by an uneducated person. To suppose that a lay-evangelist or Scripture-reader, who knows nothing of Latin or Greek, and is only familiar with his Bible, is more acceptable than an Oxford first-class man, or a Cambridge wrangler (if that first-class man knows how to preach), is a complete error. People only tolerate vulgarity and coarseness, as a rule, when they can get nothing else.

BRIEF HINTS

Having made these prefatory remarks in order to clear the way, I will now proceed to give my readers **five brief hints as to what seems to me the best method of attaining simplicity in preaching**.

1. My first hint is this—If you want to attain simplicity in preaching, **take care that you have a clear view of the subject upon which you are going to preach.** I ask your special attention to this. Of all the five hints I am about to give, this is the most important. Mind, then, when your text is chosen, that you understand it and see right through it; that you know precisely what you want to prove, what you want to teach, what you want to establish, and what you want people's minds to carry away. **If you yourself begin in a fog, you may depend upon it you will leave your people in darkness.** Cicero, one of the greatest ancient orators, said long ago, "No one can possibly speak clearly and eloquently about a subject which he does not understand"—and I am satisfied that he spoke the truth. Archbishop Whately was a very shrewd observer of human nature, and he said rightly of a vast number of preachers, that "they aimed at nothing, and they hit nothing. Like men landing on an unknown island, and setting out on a journey of exploration, they set out in ignorance, and traveled on in ignorance all the day long."

I ask all young ministers especially, to remember this first hint. I repeat most emphatically—"Take care you thoroughly understand your subject. Never choose a text of which you do not quite know what it means." Beware of taking obscure passages such as those which are to be found in unfulfilled and emblematic prophecies. If a man will continually preach to an ordinary congregation about the seals and vials and trumpets in Revelation, or about Ezekiel's temple, or about predestination, free will, and the eternal purposes of God—it will not be at all surprising to any reasonable mind if he fails to attain simplicity. I do not mean that these subjects ought not to be handled occasionally, at fit times, and before a suitable audience. All I say is, that **they are very deep subjects, about which wise Christians often disagree, and it is almost impossible to make them very simple**. We ought to see our subjects plainly, if we wish to make them simple, and there are hundreds of plain subjects to be found in God's Word.

Beware, for the same reason, of taking up what I call "fanciful subjects" and "spiritualizing texts"—and then dragging out of them meanings which the Holy Spirit never intended to put into them. There is no subject needful for the soul's health which is not to be found plainly taught and set forth in Scripture. This being the case, I think a preacher should never take a text and extract from it, as a dentist would a tooth from the jaw, something which, however true in itself, is not the plain literal meaning of the inspired words. The sermon may seem very glittering and ingenious, and his people may go away saying, "What a clever parson we have got!" But if, on examination, they can neither find the sermon in the text, nor the text in the sermon, their minds are perplexed, and they begin to think the Bible is a deep book which cannot be understood. If you want to attain simplicity, beware of spiritualizing texts.

When I speak of spiritualizing texts, let me explain what I mean. I remember hearing of a minister in a northern town, who was famous for preaching in this style. Once he gave out for his text, "He who is so impoverished that he has no oblation, chooses unto him

a tree that will not rot" (Isa. 40:20). "Here," said he, "is man by nature impoverished and undone. He has nothing to offer, in order
to make satisfaction for his soul. And what ought he to do? He
ought to choose a tree which cannot rot—even the cross of our
Lord Jesus Christ."

On another occasion, being anxious to preach on the doctrine
of indwelling sin, he chose his text out of the history of Joseph and
his brethren, and gave out the words, "The old man of whom you
spoke, is he yet alive?" (Gen. 43:27). Out of this question he ingen-
iously twisted a discourse about the infection of nature remaining
in the believer—a grand truth, no doubt, but certainly not the truth
of the passage. Such instances will, I trust, be a warning to all my
younger brethren. If you want to preach about the indwelling cor-
ruption of human nature, or about Christ crucified, you need not
seek for such far-fetched texts as those I have named. If you want
to be simple, mind you choose plain simple texts!

Furthermore, if you wish to see through your subjects thoroughly, and so to attain the foundation of simplicity, do not be
ashamed of dividing your sermons and stating your divisions. I
need hardly say this is a very vexed question. There is a morbid
dread of "firstly, secondly, and thirdly" in many quarters. The
stream of 'fashion' runs strongly against divisions, and I must
frankly confess that a lively undivided sermon is much better than
one divided in a dull, stupid, illogical way. Let every man be fully
persuaded in his own mind. He who can preach sermons which
strike and stick without divisions, by all means let him hold on his
way and persevere. But let him not despise his neighbor who divides. All I say is—if we would be simple, there must be ORDER
in a sermon as there is in an army. What wise general would mix up
artillery, infantry, and cavalry in one confused mass in the day of
battle? What giver of a banquet or dinner would dream of putting
on the table the whole of the viands at once—the soup, the fish,
the entrees, the meat, the salads, the sweets, the dessert, in one
huge dish? Such a host would hardly be thought to serve his dinner

well. Just so I say it is with sermons. By all means let there be **order**—order, whether you bring out your "firstly, secondly, or thirdly," or not—order, whether your divisions are concealed or expressed—order so carefully arranged that your points and ideas shall follow one another in beautiful regularity, like regiments marching past before the Queen on a review day in Windsor Park.

For my own part, I honestly confess that I do not think I have preached two sermons in my life without divisions. I find it of the utmost importance to make people understand, remember, and carry away what I say—and I am certain that divisions help me to do so. They are, in fact, like hooks and pegs and shelves in the mind. If you study the sermons of men who have been and are successful preachers, you will always find order, and often divisions, in their sermons. I am not a bit ashamed to say that I often read the sermons of Mr. Spurgeon. I like to gather hints about preaching from all quarters. David did not ask about the sword of Goliath—"Who made it? who polished it? what blacksmith forged it?" He said, "There is nothing like it"—for he had once used it to cut off its owner's head. Mr. Spurgeon can preach most ably, and he proves it by keeping his enormous congregation together. We ought always to examine and analyze sermons which draw people together. Now when you read Mr. Spurgeon's sermons, note how clearly and perspicuously he divides a sermon, and fills each division with beautiful and simple ideas. How easily you grasp his meaning! How thoroughly he brings before you certain great truths, that hang to you like hooks of steel, and which, once planted in your memory, you never forget!

My first point, then, if you would be simple in your preaching, is, that you must thoroughly understand your subject, and if you want to know whether you understand it, try to divide and arrange it. I can only say for myself; that I have done this ever since I have been a minister. For forty-five years I have kept note books in which I write down texts and heads of sermons for use when require. Whenever I get hold of a text, and see my way through it, I put it down and make a note of it. If I do not see my way through a text, I cannot preach on it, because I know I cannot be simple; and if I cannot be simple, I know I had better not preach at all

2. The second hint I would give is this—**Try to use in all your sermons, as far as you can—simple words.** In saying this, however, I must explain myself. When I talk of simple words, I do not mean words of only one syllable, or words which are purely Saxon. I cannot in this matter agree with Archbishop Whately. I think he goes too far in his recommendation of Saxon, though there is much truth in what he says about it. I rather prefer the saying of that wise old heathen Cicero, when he said, that orators should try to use words which are "in daily common use" among the people. Whether the words are Saxon or not—or of two or three syllables. It does not matter so long as they are words commonly used and understood by the people. Only, whatever you do, beware of what the poor shrewdly call "dictionary" words, that is, of words which are abstract, or scientific, or pedantic, or complicated, or vague, or very long. They may seem very fine, and sound very grand, but they are rarely of any use. **The most powerful and forcible words, as a rule, are very short.**

Let me say one word more to confirm what I have stated about that common fallacy of the desirableness of always using Saxon English. I would remind you that a vast number of words of other than Saxon origin are used by writers of notorious simplicity. Take, for instance, the famous work of John Bunyan, and look at the very title of it—The Pilgrim's Progress. Neither of the leading words in that title is Saxon. Would he have improved matters if he had called it "The Wayfarer's Walk"? In saying this I admit freely that words of French and Latin origin are generally inferior to Saxon; and, as a rule, I would say—use strong pure Saxon words—if you can. All I mean to say is, that you must not think it a matter of course that words cannot be good and simple if they are not of Saxon origin. In any case, beware of long words.

Dr. Gee, in his excellent book, 'Our Sermons', very ably points out **the uselessness of using long words and expressions not in common use.** For example, he says, "Talk of happiness rather than of felicity; talk of almighty rather than omnipotent; forbidden rather than proscribed; hateful rather than noxious; afterwards rather than subsequently; call out and draw forth instead of evoke and educe." We all need to be pulled up sharply on these points. It is very well to use fine words at Oxford and Cambridge, before classical hearers, and in preaching before educated audiences. But depend upon it, when you preach to ordinary congregations, the sooner you throw overboard this sort of English, and use plain common words, the better. One thing, at all events, is quite certain, **without simple words you will never attain simplicity in preaching**.

3. The third hint I would offer, if you wish to attain simplicity in preaching, is this—**Take care to aim at a simple style of composition.** I will try to illustrate what I mean. If you take up the sermons preached by that great and wonderful man Dr. Chalmers, you can hardly fail to see what an enormous number of lines you meet with without coming to a full stop. This I regard as a great mistake. It may suit Scotland, but it will never do for England. If you would attain a simple style of composition, beware of writing many lines without coming to a pause, and so **allowing the minds of your hearers to take breath**. Beware of colons and semicolons. Stick to commas and full stops, and take care to write as if you were asthmatical or short of breath. Never write or speak very long sentences or long paragraphs. Use stops frequently, and start again—and the oftener you do this, the more likely you are to attain a simple style of composition. Enormous sentences full of colons, semicolons, and parentheses, with paragraphs of two or three pages' length, are utterly fatal to simplicity. We should bear in mind that preachers have to do with hearers and not readers, and that what will "read" well will not always "speak" well. A reader of English can always help himself by looking back a few lines and refreshing his mind. A hearer of English hears once for all, and if

he loses the thread of your sermon in a long involved sentence, he very likely never finds it again.

Again, simplicity in your style of composition depends very much upon **the proper use of proverbs and pointed sentences**. This is of vast importance. Here, I think, is the value of much that you find in Matthew Henry's commentary, and Bishop Hall's Contemplations. There are some good sayings of this sort in a book not known so well as it should be, called 'Papers on Preaching'. Take a few examples of what I mean: "What we weave in time— we wear in eternity." "Hell is paved with good intentions." "Sin forsaken, is one of the best evidences of sin forgiven." "It matters little how we die—but it matters much how we live." "Meddle with no man's person—but spare no man's sin." "The street is soon clean when every one sweeps before his own door." "Lying rides on debt's back—it is hard for an empty bag to stand upright." "He who begins with prayer—will end with praise" "All is not gold that glitters." "In religion, as in business—there are no gains without pains." "In the Bible there are shallows where a lamb can wade— and depths where an elephant must swim." "One thief on the cross was saved, that none should despair—and only one, that none should presume."

Proverbial, pointed, and antithetical sayings of this kind give wonderful perspicuousness and force to a sermon. Labor to store your minds with them. Use them judiciously, and especially at the end of paragraphs, and you will find them an immense help to the attainment of a simple style of composition. But of long, involved, complicated sentences—always beware!

4. The fourth hint I will give is this: **If you wish to preach simply—use a direct style.** What do I mean by this? I mean the practice and custom of saying "I" and "you." When a man takes up this style of preaching, he is often told that he is conceited and egotistical. The result is that many preachers are never direct—and always think it very humble and modest and becoming to say "we."

But I remember good Bishop Villiers saying that "we" was a word kings and corporations should use, and they alone—but that parish clergymen should always talk of "I" and "you." I endorse that saying with all my heart. I declare I never can understand what the famous pulpit "we" means. Does the preacher who all through his sermon keeps saying "we" mean himself and the bishop? or himself and the Church? or himself and the congregation? or himself and the early Fathers? or himself and the Reformers? or himself and all the wise men in the world? or, after all, does he only mean myself, plain "John Smith" or "Thomas Jones"? If he only means himself, what earthly reason can he give for using the plural number, and not saying simply and plainly "I"? When he visits his parishioners, or sits by a sick-bed, or catechises his school, or orders bread at the baker's, or meat at the butcher's—he does not say "we," but "I." Why, then, I should like to know, can he not say "I" in the pulpit? What right has he, as a modest man, to speak for anyone but himself? Why not stand up on Sunday and say, "Reading in the Word of God, I have found a text containing such things as these, and I come to set them before you"?

Many people, I am sure, do not understand what the preacher's "we" means. The expression leaves them in a kind of fog. If you say, "**I**, the pastor of the parish, come here to talk of something that concerns your soul, something you should believe, something you should do"—you are at any rate understood. But if you begin to talk in the vague plural number of what "we" ought to do, many of your hearers do not know what you are driving at, and whether you are speaking to yourself or them. I charge and entreat my younger brethren in the ministry not to forget this point. **Do try to be as direct as possible.** Never mind what people say of you. In this particular do not imitate Chalmers, or Melville, or certain other living pulpit celebrities. Never say "we" when you mean "I." The more you get into the habit of talking plainly to the people, in the first person singular, as old Bishop Latimer did—the simpler will your sermon be, and the more easily understood. The glory of

Whitefield's sermons is their directness. But unhappily they were so badly reported, that we cannot now appreciate them.

5. The fifth and last hint I wish to give you is this: **If you would attain simplicity in preaching, you must use plenty of anecdotes and illustrations.** You must regard illustrations as windows through which light is let in upon your subject. Upon this point a great deal might be said, but the limits of a small treatise oblige me to touch it very briefly. I need hardly remind you of the example of Him who "spoke as never any man spoke"—our Lord and Savior Jesus Christ. Study the four Gospels attentively, and mark what a wealth of illustrations His sermons generally contain. How often you find figure upon figure, parable upon parable, in His discourses! There was nothing under His eyes apparently from which He did not draw lessons. The birds of the air, and the fish in the sea, the sheep, the goats, the cornfield, the vineyard, the ploughman, the sower, the reaper, the fisherman, the shepherd, the vinedresser, the woman kneading meal, the flowers, the grass, the bank, the wedding feast, the sepulcher—all were made vehicles for conveying thoughts to the minds of hearers. What are such parables as the prodigal son, the good Samaritan, the ten virgins, the king who made a marriage for his son, the rich man and Lazarus, the laborers of the vineyard, and others—what are all these but **stirring stories** that our Lord tells in order to convey some great truth to the souls of His hearers? Try to walk in His footsteps and follow His example.

If you pause in your sermon, and say, "Now I will tell you a story"—I pledge that all who are not too fast asleep will pick up their ears and listen. People like similes, illustrations, and well-told stories—and will listen to them when they will attend to nothing else. And from what countless sources we can get illustrations! Take all the book of **nature** around us. Look at the sky above and the world beneath. Look at history. Look at all the branches of **science**, at geology, at botany, at chemistry, at astronomy. What is there in heaven above or earth below from which you may not bring illustrations to throw light on the message of the gospel? Read Bishop Latimer's sermons, the most popular, perhaps, that were ever preached. Read the works of Brooks, and Watson, and Swinnock, the Puritans. How full they are of illustrations, figures, metaphors, and stories! Look at Mr. Moody's sermons. What is one secret of his popularity? He fills his sermons with pleasing stories. **He is the best speaker**, says an Arabian proverb, **who can turn the ear into an eye!**

For my part, I not only try to tell stories, but in country parishes I have sometimes put before people familiar **illustrations** which they can see. For instance—Do I want to show them that there must have been a first great cause or Being who made this world? I have sometimes taken out my watch, and have said, "Look at this watch. How well it is made! Do any of you suppose for a moment that all the screws, all the wheels, all the pins of that watch came together by accident? Would not any one say there must have been a watchmaker? And if so, it follows most surely that there must have been a Maker of the world, whose handiwork we see engraved on the face of every one of those glorious planets going their yearly rounds and keeping time to a single second. Look at the world in which you live, and the wonderful things which it contains. Will you tell me that there is no God, and that creation is the result of chance?" Or sometimes I have taken out a bunch of keys and shaken them. The whole congregation, when they hear the keys, look up. Then I say, "Would there be need of any keys if all men were perfect and honest? What does this bunch of keys show? Why, they show that the heart of man is deceitful above all things, and desperately wicked." **Illustration**, I confidently assert, is one of the best receipts for making a sermon simple, clear, perspicuous, and easily understood. Lay yourselves out for it. Pick up illustrations wherever you can. Keep your eyes open, and use them well. Happy is that preacher who has an eye for **similitudes**, and a memory stored with well-chosen stories and **illustrations**. If he is a real man of God, and knows how to deliver a sermon, he will never preach to bare walls and empty benches.

But I must add a word of caution. There is a proper way of telling stories. If a man cannot tell stories naturally—he had better **not** tell them at all. Illustration, again, after all I have said in its favor, may be carried too far. I remember a notable instance of this in the case of the great Welsh preacher, Christmas Evans. There is in print a sermon of his about the wonderful miracle that took place in Gadara, when devils took possession of the swine, and the whole herd ran down violently into the sea. He paints it so minutely that it really becomes ludicrous by reason of the words put in the mouth of the swine-herders who told their master of the loss he had sustained. "Oh! sir," says one, "the pigs have all gone!" "But," says the master, "where have they gone?" "They have run down into the sea." "But who drove them down?" "Oh! sir, that wonderful man." "Well, what sort of a man was he? What did he do?" "Why, sir, he came and talked such strange things, and the whole herd ran suddenly down the steep place into the sea." "What, the old black boar and all?" "Yes, sir, the old black boar has gone too; for as we looked round, we just saw the end of his tail going over the cliff." Now that is going to an extreme. So, again, Dr. Guthrie's admirable sermons are occasionally so overlaid with illustrations as to remind one of cake made almost entirely of plums and containing hardly any flour. Put plenty of color and picture into your sermon by all means. Draw sweetness and light from all sources and from all creatures—from the heavens and the earth, from history, from science. But after all there is a limit. You must be careful how you use color—lest you do as much harm as good. Do not put on color by **spoonfuls**, but with a **brush**. This caution remembered, you will find color an immense aid in the attainment of simplicity and perspicuousness in preaching.

FIVE KEY POINTS

And now bear in mind that my five points are these—

1. If you want to attain simplicity in preaching, you must **have a clear knowledge of what you are going to preach**.

2. If you would attain simplicity in preaching, you must **use simple words**.

3. If you would attain simplicity in preaching, you must **seek to acquire a simple style of composition**, with short sentences and as few colons and semicolons as possible.

4. If you would attain simplicity in preaching, **aim at directness**.

5. If you would attain simplicity in preaching, **make abundant use of illustration and anecdote**.

Let me add to all this one plain word of **application**. You will never attain simplicity in preaching without **plenty of work**—pains and trouble, I say emphatically, pains and trouble. When Turner, the great painter, was asked by some one how it was he mixed his colors so well, and what it was that made them so different from those of other artists—"Mix them? mix them? mix them? Why, with brains, sir." I am persuaded that, in preaching, **little can be done except by trouble and by pains**.

I have heard that a young and careless clergyman once said to Richard Cecil, "I think I need more faith." "No," said the wise old man—"you need more work. You need more pains. You must not think that God will do work for you—though He is ready to do it by you." I entreat my younger brethren to remember this. I beg them to make time for their composition of sermons, to take trouble and to exercise their brains by reading. Only mind that you read what is useful.

I would not have you spend your time in reading the early church Fathers in order to help your preaching. They are very useful in their way, but there are many things more useful in modern writers, if you choose them discreetly.

Read good models, and become familiar with good specimens of simplicity in preaching. As your best model, take the English Bible. If you speak the language in which that is written, you will speak well. Read John Bunyan's immortal work, the Pilgrim's progress. Read it again and again, if you wish to attain simplicity in preaching. Do not be above reading the Puritans. Some of them no doubt are heavy. Goodwin and Owen are very heavy, though excellent artillery in position. Read such books as Baxter, and Watson, and Traill, and Flavel, and Charnock, and Hall, and Henry. They are, to my mind, models of the best simple English spoken in old times. Remember, however, that language alters with years. They spoke English, and so do we, but their style was different from ours. Read beside them the best models of modern English that you can get at. I believe the best English writer for the last hundred years was William Cobbett, the political Radical. I think he wrote the finest simple Saxon-English the world has ever seen. In the present day I do not know a greater master of tersely spoken Saxon-English than John Bright. Among old political orators, the speeches of Lord Chatham and Patrick Henry, the American, are models of good English. Last, but not least, never forget that, next to the Bible, there is nothing in the English language which, for combined simplicity, perspicuousness, eloquence, and power, can be compared with some of the great speeches in Shakespeare. Models of this sort must really be studied, and studied "with brains," too, if you wish to attain a good style of composition in preaching. On the other hand, do not be above talking to the poor, and visiting your people from house to house. Sit down with your people by the fireside, and exchange thoughts with them on all subjects. Find out how they think and how they express themselves, if you want them to understand your sermons. By so doing you will insensibly learn much. You will be continually picking up modes of thought, and get notions as to what you should say in your pulpit.

A humble country clergyman was once asked "whether he studied the fathers." The worthy man replied, that he had little opportunity of studying the fathers, as they were generally out in the fields when he called. But he studied the mothers more, because he often found them at home—and he could talk to them.

Wittingly or unwittingly, the good man hit a nail right on the head. We must talk to our people when we are out of church—if we would understand how to preach to them in the church.

1. I will only say, in conclusion, that whatever we preach, or whatever pulpit we occupy, whether we preach simply or not, whether we preach written or extempore, we ought to aim not merely at letting off fireworks, but at **preaching that which will do lasting good to souls!** Let us beware of fireworks in our preaching. "Beautiful" sermons, "brilliant" sermons, "clever" sermons, "popular" sermons, are often sermons which have no effect on the congregation, and do not draw men to Jesus Christ. Let us aim so to preach, that what we say may really come home to men's minds and consciences and hearts, and make them think and consider.

2. All the simplicity in the world can do no good, unless you **preach the simple gospel of Jesus Christ so fully and clearly that everybody can understand it.** If 'Christ crucified' has not His rightful place in your sermons, and 'sin' is not exposed as it should be, and your people are not plainly told what they ought to believe, and be, and do—**your preaching is of no use!**

3. All the simplicity in the world, again, is useless without **a good lively delivery.** If you bury your head in your bosom, and mumble over your manuscript in a dull, monotonous, droning way, like a bee in a bottle, so that people cannot understand what you

are speaking about—your preaching will be in vain. Depend upon it, delivery is not sufficiently attended to in our Church. In this, as in everything else connected with the science of preaching, I consider the Church of England is sadly deficient. I know that I began preaching alone in the New Forest, and nobody ever told me what was right or wrong in the pulpit. The result was that the first year of my preaching was a series of experiments. We get no help in these matters at Oxford and Cambridge. The utter lack of any proper training for the pulpit is one great blot and defect in the system of the Church of England.

4. Above all, let us never forget that all the simplicity in the world is useless without **prayer for the outpouring of the Holy Spirit,** and the grant of God's blessing, and a life corresponding in some measure to what we preach. Be it ours to have an earnest desire for the souls of men, while we seek for simplicity in preaching the gospel of Jesus Christ, and let us never forget to accompany our sermons by holy living and fervent prayer!

Also from Benediction Books ...
Wandering Between Two Worlds: Essays on Faith and Art
Anita Mathias
Benediction Books, 2007
152 pages
ISBN: 0955373700

In these wide-ranging lyrical essays, Anita Mathias writes, in lush, lovely prose, of her naughty Catholic childhood in Jamshedpur, India; her large, eccentric family in Mangalore, a sea-coast town converted by the Portuguese in the sixteenth century; her rebellion and atheism as a teenager in her Himalayan boarding school, run by German missionary nuns, St. Mary's Convent, Nainital; and her abrupt religious conversion after which she entered Mother Teresa's convent in Calcutta as a novice. Later rich, elegant essays explore the dualities of her life as a writer, mother, and Christian in the United States-- Domesticity and Art, Writing and Prayer, and the experience of being "an alien and stranger" as an immigrant in America, sensing the need for roots.

About the Author

Anita Mathias is the author of *Wandering Between Two Worlds: Essays on Faith and Art.* She has a B.A. and M.A. in English from Somerville College, Oxford University, and an M.A. in Creative Writing from the Ohio State University, USA. Anita won a National Endowment of the Arts fellowship in Creative Nonfiction in 1997. She lives in Oxford, England with her husband, Roy, and her daughters, Zoe and Irene.

Visit Anita at http://www.anitamathias.com.

The Church That Had Too Much
Anita Mathias
Benediction Books, 2010
52 pages
ISBN: 9781849026567

The Church That Had Too Much was very well-intentioned. She wanted to love God, she wanted to love people, but she was both hampered by her muchness and the abundance of her possessions, and beset by ambition, power struggles and snobbery. Read about the surprising way The Church That Had Too Much began to resolve her problems in this deceptively simple and enchanting fable.

The Meek Shall Inherit The Earth
Anita Mathias
Benediction Books, 2013
38 pages
ISBN: 9781781393956

"Blessed are the meek, for they shall inherit the earth," Jesus says in his most puzzling Beatitude. Puzzling, because, if we are honest, it does not feel true to our experience. So do the meek inherit the earth? Is this true? Or isn't it? In The Meek Shall Inherit the Earth, an extended meditation on the power of gentleness, Anita Mathias grapples with this mystifying Beatitude..

Visit Anita at http://www.anitamathias.com

Francesco, Artist of Florence: The Man Who Gave Too Much
Anita Mathias
Benediction Books, 2014
52 pages (full colour)
ISBN: 978-1781394175

In this lavishly illustrated book by Anita Mathias, Francesco, artist of Florence, creates magic in pietre dure, inlaying precious stones in marble in life-like "paintings." While he works, placing lapis lazuli birds on clocks, and jade dragonflies on vases, he is purely happy. However, he must sell his art to support his family. Francesco, who is incorrigibly soft-hearted, cannot stand up to his haggling customers. He ends up almost giving away an exquisite jewellery box to Signora Farnese's bambina, who stands, captivated, gazing at a jade parrot nibbling a cherry. Signora Stallardi uses her daughter's wedding to cajole him into discounting his rainbowed marriage chest. His old friend Girolamo bullies him into letting him have the opulent table he hoped to sell to the Medici almost at cost. Carrara is raising the price of marble; the price of gems keeps rising. His wife is in despair. Francesco fears ruin.

* * *

Sitting in the church of Santa Maria Novella at Mass, very worried, Francesco hears the words of Christ. The lilies of the field and the birds of the air do not worry, yet their Heavenly Father looks after them. As He will look after us. He resolves not to worry. And as he repeats the prayer the Saviour taught us, Francesco resolves to forgive the friends and neighbours who repeatedly put their own interests above his. But can he forgive himself for his own weakness, as he waits for the eternal city of gold whose walls are made of jasper, whose gates are made of pearls, and whose foundations are sapphire, emerald, ruby and amethyst? There time and money shall be no more, the lion shall live with the lamb, and we shall dwell trustfully together. Francesco leaves Santa Maria Novella, resolving to trust the One who told him to live like the lilies and the birds, deciding to forgive those who haggled him into bad bargains--while making a little resolution for the future.